JustMeQi

Copyright © 2020 by Warren Henderson.

ISBN-978-1-6455-0820-5

All rights reserved. No part of this book may be reproduced or transmitted in any form or by any means, electronic or mechanical, including photocopying, recording, or by any information storage and retrieval system, without permission in writing from the copyright owner.

The views expressed in this work are solely those of the author and do not necessarily reflect the views of the publisher, and the publisher hereby disclaims any responsibility for them.

Matchstick Literary
1-888-306-8885
orders@matchliterary.com

JustMeQi

Just Words for A Just Spirit

Warren L. Henderson, Jr.

Cover Design © 2014 Leah Sophia Chang
facebook: facebook.com/suntreeriverdesign
blogger: suntreeriverdesign.blogspot.com/
urbanities: preservationproject.blogspot.com/
linkedin: linkedin.com/in/suntreeriver

CONTENTS

Praise for JustMeQi 7
Disclaimer 8
About the Author 9
To Contact the Author 11
Acknowledgements 13

What is JustMeQi ? 15
    Understanding my Justice 15
Why JustMeQi ? 24
    Understanding my Just life 24
Manifesting Justice 28
    Let Life Astonish You 28
Looking For JustMeQi 31
    Some people who live a Just life, benefiting others: 31
What's Next? 47
    Where will you go from here for your Just Qi? 47
Take A Step 50
    Prime the pump of compassion by taking a leap of faith 50
    Sample list of organizations for ideas that fit your Qi 55

Acknowledgements 57
    People who contributed stories for JustMeQi 57

PRAISE FOR *JUSTMEQI*

JustMeQi is a wonderful testament to the difference each of us can make in the world. It will be an inspiration to all who value social justice but don't quite know where to begin. Read it with an open heart and begin your own path to achieving self-fulfillment through a life dedicated to love and service.

~ **Carol Cujec, Ph.D., Lecturer in Humanities at Cal State University San Marcos, California and Point Loma Nazarene University, San Diego, California**

Many thanks, Warren, for sharing this pre-release. It reveals the beauty of your soul and your dedication to making this a better world. Let's talk a bit about your accomplishments during our Faith, Order and Witness Committee meeting tomorrow. I also appreciate the artistic talents of Leah Sophia Chang that were used for the cover.

~ **Rev. John George Huber, retired minister in the Lutheran Church, Missouri Synod**

Disclaimer

The author and publisher shall not be liable for the misuse of this material. This book is strictly for informational and educational purposes.

Disclaimer: The purpose of this book is to educate and entertain. The author and/or publisher do not warrant that the information contained in this report is fully complete and shall not be responsible for any errors or omissions. Nor do they guarantee that anyone following these techniques, suggestions, tips, ideas, or strategies will become successful in any way. The author and/or publisher shall have neither liability nor responsibility to anyone with respect to any loss or damage caused or alleged to be caused, directly or indirectly by the information contained in this book.

ABOUT THE AUTHOR

Warren Henderson is an emerging author of positive, motivating and entertaining material like *JustMeQi*. He is well read and has traveled extensively. Originally from Union, New Jersey, he now resides in Bonita California. Having taught religious education and coordinated many liturgical and non-liturgical programs since 1980 in several Southern California Dioceses, he presently facilitates multiple *Faith In Action Team* activities in the San Diego Diocese. His mission in life is to be of service and to continue to produce and share informative and uplifting books, articles and practices. For more information, please log on to *JustMeQi*.com.

    Warren worked as director of Electronics & Computer Technology and center dean and is currently an associate professor of ECT. Prior to teaching, Warren spent more than 25 years as CEO and chief R&D consulting engineer for HENDERSON COMMUNICATIONS LABORATORIES. Warren was also a contributing member of multiple Telecommunications Industry Association (TIA) industry standards implementation committees and has been recognized as an Insightful Entrepreneur by the Entrepreneur Association of Southern California.

    For decades, Warren practiced Qi Gong and researched a myriad of practices engaging the union of mind, body, and spirit (such as Tai Chi, Energy Medicine, and Neurolinguistics). Threading these aspects of life with fundamental Christian principles led to conceptualizing this way of life as *JustMeQi*.

TO CONTACT THE AUTHOR

If you would like more information about this book or the practice of *JustMeQi*, or would like to contact the author regarding speaking engagements, please visit www.*JustMeQi*.com. This website is dedicated to providing visitors with new and exciting approaches to expanding their personal joy through service. You may also write to *JustMeQi*@hotmail.com.

JustMeQi is dedicated to men and women in any form of service around the world.

ACKNOWLEDGEMENTS

Much of the motivation for this book came from my parents, Warren, Sr. and Marie—not, however, in the way they spoke with us but in the way they lived their American and Christian values. In combination, the Benedictine nuns of Saint James School, Springfield, New Jersey and the Marist Brothers at Union Catholic High School, provided a solid foundation for my faith along with a constructive practice that enabled open-mindedness, embracing universal values and differences.

My expression of appreciation would not be complete without acknowledging the communities of St. Patrick Church in Moreno Valley, California, and St. James Church in Solana Beach, California, for the opportunity to minister within a variety of parish programs.

WHAT IS *JUSTMEQI*?

Understanding my Justice.

JustMeQi is a lifestyle of transformed people. Individuals with a soul philosophy (Chi, Qi, Xi, "Chee") of expanded commitment to ethical, well-grounded (justified) social ministry practice *JustMeQi*. This lifestyle implements life-changing concepts that enable one to study, explore and experience our call to care for each other and our world at large (poor or not, vulnerable or not). Individually and collectively, living is thought-provoking and stimulating when we allow it to involve us.

Qi or Chi is, in traditional Chinese culture, an active component of any living thing. Frequently used when referencing our natural energy or life force. Literally translated as breath, Qi is the key principle in Chinese and various esoteric forms of spirituality and alternative medicine practices.

Concepts similar to Qi can be found throughout history and in many societies—most notably: Hawaiian and Hebrew cultures, as well as Hindu and Tibetan Buddhism religions. Within Western philosophy, Qi is known as our vital energy.

The *JustMeQi* lifestyle practitioners maintain a personal, mindful, responsibility to be involved in advancing a more just world.

Generally speaking most adults feel that discussing social *Justice* (in any form) is akin to social conversations regarding religion and politics—"don't broach the subject unless you are absolutely certain all other parties are in full agreement!"

JustMeQi lifestyle practitioners acquire a working education regarding resource needs and accessibility. They seek out situations to thoughtfully discuss the information with diverse peoples and develop a consistent sense of community building. Often they will explore traditional and original meditation and prayer experiences.

The Just in *JustMeQi* refers to any number of proper variations of fair, impartial, unprejudiced, correct, moral, ethical, valid or balanced.

We hope that, guided by truth, reason, Justice, and fairness, we will be just in our handling of challenging conditions. Being just entails living in harmony with equitable principles.

To experience or feel the world around you in its entirety rather than as successions of segregated points of interest is to engage your Qi.

JustMeQi

> *JustMeQi is the psychology of taking responsibility for living your own Just life, in all aspects of your life, without imposing Just behaviors on others.*

Your mark on the world shouldn't be the mark a dog leaves on his territory. As part of a society—the community of human beings—every individual contributes in some manner to the realm beyond their immediate line-of-sight (so to speak).

If you are inclined to read this, you are probably familiar with the Butterfly Effect. Coined by Edward Lorenz, it is his reference to a proposition that a hurricane on one part of the globe can be traced to the fluttering wings of a butterfly weeks earlier in another part of the world. While the concept may seem a bit overstated, it doesn't take much of an imagination to see how a series of otherwise diverse actions or conditions can ultimately have an impact on a given situation or circumstance. So it is with individual creatures—certainly we "higher realm" beings. Acting, or choosing not to act, in a particular way or towards a particular individual or within a particular event, can ripple through disparate connections to effect life a long ways off.

We live in a world where there is a serious hunger for love. The pain and loneliness are something that we all have experienced. The deprived may be right in your own community. When we have the strength of character to see them, we can find the strength of heart to assist them.

We live in a world that teaches us that there is something wrong with us. We build the illusion that some people are faultless as they are and that there is something wrong with others who are less than perfect. Often we attack to show that we are better, stronger, or otherwise superior to cover that we think we are bad.

In reality, we are perfect just as we are. Our whole culture is living in disconnection from ourselves and one another. As a society, we have to get connected to the reality of our individual and collective soundness. As role models, we need to relate to our children that they are okay. When our children accept themselves and one another they can transform this situation.

JustMeQi is more than legal or moral Justice. It is about a level of living
—of loving—that is higher than quid pro quo.
The "JustMe" experience allows you to enjoy the happiness
and joy of giving love—freely and without expectation.

Morals are the rules that govern which actions are right and which are wrong. A set of morals can be for all of society or an individual's beliefs. Sometimes a moral can be gleaned from a story told or a personal experience. Collective conventions regarding "right" and "wrong" aspects of living for all of society are the moral foundations of laws and individual conscience.

Some listed morals include various versions of:

- Tell the truth
- Do not cheat
- Have humility
- Be forgiving
- Be accountable
- Keep your promises
- Morals in Literature
- Keep your self-control
- Do not commit adultery
- Be tolerant of differences
- Have respect for yourself
- Do not bear false witness
- Do not vandalize property
- Honor your father and mother
- Treat others as you want to be treated
- Be loyal
- Do not kill
- Do not steal
- Do not judge
- Seek *Justice*
- Be generous
- Be dependable
- Respect others
- Do not gossip
- Have patience
- Have courage
- Have integrity
- Serve mankind
- Be trustworthy
- Take responsibility

Justice is choosing actions according to their objective right or wrong consequence, rather than a subjective evaluation or judgment strictly to law.

Justice is about the balance of values, needs and consequences. Not as cut-and-dry as legal versus illegal or moral, amoral and immoral, Justice is often complex.

In the case of your own Qi, an apparent conundrum of absolute and relative choices must often include appraisals overlooked by simpler apparent elements.

> *Within social justice teaching, the aim is level sharing of all groups, in a society that acts cooperatively to serve mutual essentials. Justice, beyond legalism, is a vision of civilization that is equitable as regards wealth, opportunity, privilege, and physical safety.*

The point here is that when we look closer at the purpose of our spiritual work and growth, we can see that the path of life is not only about eliminating our own suffering and securing our own happiness. As long as that's all we're seeking, we won't get very far. Our spiritual path grows valuable when transforming ourselves in the deepest ways becomes a personal imperative, with intended consequences beyond ourselves.

JustMeQi means we realize that our lives are not merely our personal possession to conduct as we see fit—but rather, that we are accountable to the greater world in everything we do.

When we view our personal obligation as evolving for the greater good, we find that we have an infinite energy, intention, passion and strength to tackle the trials that challenge us on our path.

Consider, as well, how insignificant those previously overwhelming personal fears, uncertainties and conflicts become because our focus is now on something bigger than "Me."

When we change how we view our life context and behold the bigger picture of being, our individual concerns fade in the ever sharpening enriched vision.

JustMeQi means living—choosing to act—considerate of the needs of others without being judgmental of their deservedness. How many times have you been told "it's not all about you?" Well, it isn't. Concede, rather, that your entitlement is really "about" your right to participate in the grand journey of advancement of your Qi. Ultimately this abandonment of self-concern will lead to the deep inner peace and joy you've been seeking all along.

Once you embrace this thought, *JustMeQi* leads to sharing your experiences and results from this adventure so other people can know that they can do it too. Talking about it or attending lectures isn't enough. Hearing is not listening, nor is it understanding. *JustMeQi* entails listening attentively. That's when you hear the most unexpected.

Sometimes, grabbing someone by the hand and taking them along (or going along with them) is the best way to share experiences.

Do you want them to know your world? You DO want to know their world!

Do you genuinely believe "others should know what you know"? Then give them a chance!

> *The expectation of trickle-down economics was that when the proverbial glass was full, the rising wealth within it would overflow, benefitting the poor. Instead, greed keeps making the glass bigger, providing nothing for the poor.*

It is fairly well understood that we become our habitual thoughts. When unremitting thoughts of pessimism are replaced with reassuring and inspiring attitudes, the effort yields a reciprocal turnaround in the world around you. The same holds true for the larger world.

Think of it—you can create radical results in the world by the way you live your life—positively interfacing with all aspects of the world. Justice in life is a choice. Balance vs. restlessness, harmony vs. conflict, poverty vs. abundance are all choices we need to make. Inner peace is not a result of circumstance. It is a choice.

There are many misperceptions about *JustMeQi* that stop a lot of would-be champions in their quest. It's not necessary to be "perfect" or to "know it all" or to be "enlightened." Just be yourself—willing to share you with others. Like most people, you are knowledgeable about amazing things, if you shared that understanding with others, you could influence, help and positively impact other lives.

Spiritual growth and transformation challenges us so deeply that we often choose to continue existing in our insignificance, rather than gamble on what happens if our smallness dies forever. In the big picture, it isn't only our own anguish that we are perpetuating. Instead, the suffering of the entire human race is really ours to effect.

While you may be thinking that your growth and evolution alone isn't enough to change the human race. Consider that any one of us can have a powerful effect on the world around us. Think, too, about the concept that we have an obligation to the whole.

What if the entire human endeavor, the advancement of society itself, depended on your willingness to stand outside your own envelope? Consider the choices you make every day. Those decisions are either furthering the betterment of the whole or its detriment.

Right now, it seems that what's in store for us all depends on our commitment to evolve. *JustMeQi* empowers your choice in acting in alignment with the greatest social good.

WHY JUSTMEQI ?

Understanding my Just life.

If freedom is to be significant in a civilized culture, there needs to be a fusion self-determinations and self-control within a hierarchy of responsibility.

Justice at any level can only be secured while the journey towards *Justice* for all life endures. For example, food for me includes health for everyone. Poverty isn't as cut-and-dry as homelessness or foreign countries.

For instance, across our country and even in our back yards, people are working in factories and plants under unsafe or unhealthy conditions, earning miserable wages. At the same time, corporations rake in sacrilegiously high salaries and profits for stockholders. Thinking as an individual, "I need to promote the *Just* precedence of labor- and human-rights over unreasonable corporate profits. Unless or until I act, nothing will change."

In *JustMeQi,* I can see that peaceable coexistence for all people is expressed through wholly ethical values, a respect for all life and founded on a lifestyle based on my own inner harmony. Having embraced a practice of compassion and rationality, I experience an emerging to the wisdom of living in a way that is not only free from causing injury, but recognizes, as well, the joy and happiness that comes with such a life. To understand what it means to live a healthy and peaceful life, I need to develop personal harmony and strive towards health for all humanity. Often we rightfully hear that "Peace for one must be peace for all. Prosperity for one must be abundance for all."

Warren L. Henderson, Jr.

> *Character is not defined merely by an idea a person holds. Instead, strength of character is determined by the intensity with which he embraces it.*

The solutions to the world's problems already exist! I can work to solve our problems based on the way I think of myself. New personal experiences reveal to me where beliefs of the past no longer apply. When that happens, I owe it to myself and the world to revise my thinking!

Love is the most powerful force on the planet. Learning to love the world is the greatest love of all. A positive relationship with the world can help you live a life that shines.

Wars have been waged, and temples have been built in the name of love. One key to involved living is learning to see beyond your experience in the world—to see some of the darkness balanced with all the brightness around us. Loving truly, as one of the most powerful forces on the planet, includes acting justly on that love in dealing with less-than-loving forces.

Being in love with humanity is not about walking around boasting your *JustMeQi*. It's about advocating for your neighbor—stepping out of your comfort zone, and into your Qi power—so you can truly contribute to the world.

Learning how to love in a way it is needed is one of the most powerful actions we can take. Acting to impact one's ability to thrive, or even survive, is *JustMeQi*. Develop an optimal, thriving relationship with the world starting NOW!

JustMeQi means savoring life, not controlling existence; to join not separate; grounded in poverty & humility. It means you can never know enough or do enough for enough. Therefore, be determined to change the world from the inside out—from inside you!

Starting your day with meditation is like limbering up your soul in advance of the workout you will encounter moving through your life. It sets you up for compassion, energy, excitement and strength of heart.

JustMeQi: A philosophy engaging entrepreneurial approaches to solve the world's toughest challenges—serving the poor with choice, not charity, and a significant potential to grow—is a *Just* way of life. A peacefulness follows a *JustMeQi* decision because it is right.

JustMeQi means actively embracing life's challenges. *Just* people acknowledge that life is full of good and bad, positive and negative, yet they cultivate a mindset that uses strategies to move the world forward.

Until now, we understood that disease and conflict, are inevitable in our lives. In reality, we are naturally healthy, peaceful beings. Embracing *JustMeQi* concepts exposes us to the veracity of this principle enabling us to attain this state. In essence, global consciousness, itself, is impacted as we modify our philosophy and alter our beliefs.

The abundance that comes with living in peace demands inner harmony as our personal priority, contentment, good fortune and health will follow when we commit to developing this pathway to transformation. Meditating at least once a day enables a deeper understanding of who we are. Engaging ourselves teaches us to develop a capacity to live and express an expanded level of awareness.

More than simply sustaining personal mental attitude, *JustMeQi*'s health facet includes eating nourishing foods – in keeping with the preservation of life, nature and the planet.

Not to be overlooked, either, is the *JustMeQi* connection to consciousness that includes sustaining earth, nature and all life. Qi—the circulating life energy that in Chinese philosophy is thought to be inherent in all things—consists of energy, the 5 fundamental elements (atoms, molecules, minerals, foods and life forms), vibrations and rhythms. In nature (as in physics) these elements continually cycle to and through each other creating and recreating. The mind is the keeper of the Qi. Your connection to your mind and your world is your consciousness.

MANIFESTING JUSTICE

Let Life Astonish You

Asserting that you can forgive, but will not forget, is only masking that you will not forgive. Forgetting doesn't mean a lesson hasn't been learned, it means not dwelling on the pain it caused.

JustMeQi people practice bestowing a second chance by seeking compassionate ways to reconcile as opposed to behaviors of retribution. Not unlike "Tikkun Olam" (a Hebrew phrase meaning "repairing or healing the world" and suggests humanity's shared responsibility to reconcile, and transform the world), *JustMeQi* depends on our ability to serve a greater purpose than our own to heal the world.

Think about it, if—day after day—your life is made up of things you don't believe in, or habits without design, you hinder potentials for original, fresh and enriched existence.

Given this limited time to carry out any durability to your existence, consider what motivates you, brings you joy or touches your spirit and develop that connection. Whether it is an action, someone or something that invigorates you, acknowledge that importance. Set aside the unimportant. Make aspects of your life consequential enough to brighten your *Qi*. Then decide that you want to establish or increase your *Justice Qi*. As simple as it sounds, it is a commitment that requires commitment. Like any other goal in life, once you are clear about *JustMeQi,* and you give yourself specific ambitions to develop it, your accomplishment is assured.

Justice is the key to the developmental rise of humanity because it enables us to bond to and with each other.

Adhering to personal *Justice*, as in *JustMeQi*, we nurture fidelity, healthy-humility, diligence and humanity itself. In doing so, we transform more than ourselves; we change society and the world, inaugurating in the human race new ways of living at every level, including an inviolate regard for social action.

JustMeQi is the empowerment of individual beings in our great consciousness. Its goal is to channel compassion and wisdom into radical, revered acts of service in whatever ways I am called.

The passion within us to strive for peace is *JustMeQi*. So, too, is the ambition to have abundance, the urge to laugh and the instinct to blossom with the fullness of life. *Justice* is—or should be—a primary goal in our everyday life. That core feeling of awareness, transforming me away from harming any living being, enables me to see the intrinsic beauty of everything.

JustMeQi becomes the prevailing energy within us for bringing about dynamic change in the world through goodwill and harmony. We can step up and apply *Justice* in our daily life through the intensity of heart and spirit.

Practicing *JustMeQi,* you don't internalize the anger, rage or wrath of the world around you. Instead, extricating yourself from inequality, dishonesty and other injustices in life will enable you to live logically and justly. Avoiding reactiveness impacts how you experience the world and your personal reality.

JustMeQi, as a personal moral justice life-style, looks at "personal mission" dynamics that shape consciousness and the prospect for collective action in our communities and the world.

LOOKING FOR JUSTMEQI

Some people who live a Just life, benefiting others:

The process of working toward a just goal, participating in a just and challenging activity, is as important to well-being as its attainment.

If your ultimate goal is serving via charitable organizations, the most important step to realizing that role can be getting such foundations to become aware of you in the first place.

Like any other career position, you will need more than simply a résumé that includes aid-related jobs. A profound CV that ignites interest in you, your talents and experience(s) significantly enhances your likelihood of getting interviewed.

The reality is that recruiters & hiring managers for aid organizations often have to sort through an enormous number of résumés. Unless you are staunchly committed to your *JustMeQi*, if your résumé is in the pile, your prospects for a specific assignment with a selected aid agency can be relatively slim.

Warren L. Henderson, Jr.

Look into the eyes of the person before you or the heart pictured in your mind. Some will see their creator, others will see their chosen prophet still others will see a child (perhaps their own). Now you are a person who will not harm others.

Gang Prevention—Gang Intervention—Post Detention Reentry

One summer morning in 2012 several prison ministers gathered at Donovan prison in San Diego County, California, to hear recognized community leader Father Greg Boyle address about 300 prisoners. His talk covered various aspects of his experience living with gangs in Los Angeles and steps he's offered gang members towards a better life. He peppered his philosophies with more than 25 years of stories recounting the glory of success and the grief of not. Many of us had read Father Boyle's book, "Tattoos on the Heart", and even met him in person at previous presentations. Everyone in attendance was moved.

Over lunch, following the speech a dozen of the ministers met offsite and began planning an organization that would duplicate Father Greg's Los Angeles work here in San Diego. Over the next four months, we met to brainstorm and form a business plan.

Several team members visited his **Homeboy Industries** facilities, as well as similar organizations, including **Taller San Jose** in Santa Ana, California.

Eventually we defined a mission statement, recognized a president and selected a board of directors. **Rise Up Industries** was born. Those early-on men organized a tattoo removal association, several residential possibilities and micro-businesses to provide job opportunities for men being released from prison.

With an eye towards the "why are these men entering prison to begin with?"—Gangs—the **RUI** mission plan includes deterring the entry of youngsters into the gang lifestyle by presenting positive alternatives. Rescuing gang members before the criminal life takes hold, is a big part of that mission as well.

> *Being a "home artist" means the walls of her house are her canvas. Emblazoned wherever you turn—via loving images and words—are spirit-filled phrases of welcoming with classic "Charity Starts at Home" and "Family is Everything" texts.*
>
> **~Romela C**

Having been raised in a family with 7 brothers (not to mention countless—equally prolific—aunts, uncles and cousins), Romela is no stranger to sharing. To this day, she provides a roof over the heads of various welcomed family and extended-family members.

JustMeQi is far from a mandate that you find a foreign country or even venture away from home to promote justice. Every person you touch is an opportunity to share that warmth and growth that comes with "doing an unsolicited good deed." Consider, too, that when you are affecting others, you are providing examples or mentoring that can be passed on as well.

For Romela, her aspiration is to subtly plant sentiments in the minds and hearts of visitors that they will embrace in their own lives and impart to others. Extending the Saint Francis of Assisi philosophy, "…not all words are spoken."

As one walks around Romela's home, you see:

TOGETHER WE MAKE A FAMILY

Love sees no borders (beneath a sketch of the world)

Home is everything that makes us feel: Beautiful, Safe, Loved

The fondest memories are made when gathered around the table

Together is a wonderful place to be.

Painted above the front door to be read as you exit the home:

Remember who you are & Return with Honor.

JustMeQi means my life is neither constant frivolity nor anguished with anxieties. My life is received as a gift, not a burden, where the key to bliss is laughter.

~Amy M

It seems to me like there is a real need to share our being with others. Surely, the work that I am called to is a privilege. God gave me two hands—to do work—and since I am able, then things like working with *Bread of Life Rescue Mission*[1] are how I will use them. My niece thinks of me as someone who get antsy. I always need to be doing something. I can't sit still.

Growing up I watched my mom in our home. I heard the words she spoke as well as the life she lived. I saw a woman that was fully human with her own set of weaknesses and flaws, and also a woman fully given to faith. I never had to struggle with a perceived split identity. Mom was who she was, or more accurately, who she is.

Ours is a big family. There are plenty of occasions to help. People didn't always ask… it was necessary to recognize the need that needed to be fulfilled. I would like to think that I learned a thing or two from observing my mom. Volunteering isn't something that came as an epiphany—it's a quality I grew into.

On the subject of service mistakes or regrets: "I wouldn't change anything about who I am or what I've done. Every experience is an opportunity to learn." What I have learned, too, is that I am a worker, not an organizer. Christy B. coordinates volunteers with community project needs and I show-up.

It never ceases to amaze me how much time and effort some people are prepared to put into helping those in need. That said, there are plenty more out there who could help—just a little bit—to ensure that life gets better for those who need it the most.

Serving others was not a new concept for Doctor True, but certainly whetted his appetite for helping to make a difference and for working with outreach organizations. In one case the channel was The West Indies Mission, later renamed World Team.

~Doctor Wayne True, MD
(in his own words)

Throughout my time in medical school, opportunities included serving in rural Kentucky and Peoria, Illinois to treat patients from Haiti with severe congenital heart disease.

(True has been a member of many medical teams over the years—14 trips in all—to areas that have no running water, no purified water, extremely high parasite burden and chronic disease.)

We found a Catholic Church organization that had a Food For Work program. They traded staple products—flower, rice, beans, oil—for work in building a road in and out of the area. Ultimately, this enabled them to get their coffee products out of the valley and to the market. It was the first step in an ongoing public health and hospital program that was going up about 20 miles away.

This was not a unique approach to helping the community. The program was patterned after the Albert Schweitzer hospital in another area of Haiti.

After our children were a bit older, a call came for services in a very rural area of Peru from a pastor with "Christian Emergency Relief Services." The trip was expected to be dangerous—traveling on rapids, boats overturn, and people get lost in the thick jungles. However, they had an epidemic of what turned out to be rabies. Apparently a community of bats had become rabid and migrated up the Amazon. They needed to bring netting to cover the windows, keeping the bats out at night and a doctor to administer immunizations.

A year later (1997), as we returned to the village to do a follow-up assessment, the people came running out screaming at the top of their lungs. For a moment, not knowing that we were being greeted with joy and gratitude, I thought "This is how it all ends!"

My latest project was running for Congress. I wanted to be of service to our country. I've been saddened and horrified by some of the changes that I've seen in the medical community and in government. I thought I could actually make a difference here. Even though I didn't win the nomination, I'm not done yet.

JustMeQi *means answering the question: "How do we respond to the Christ who shows us the character of a Creator who offers the full richness of creation for all? What would our life look like if we saw ourselves called from our 'boats on the lake shore' to walk with Him?"*

~**Amanda and Murray M**

Well, however awkward or surprising as it may seem, these are not theoretical questions—Christ's timeless challenge to us is as real to us as the breath that at this very moment sustains our life. These questions demand answers ... yes, from you ... and me!

I recently heard a priest turn another one of my trusted conventions on its head: "a business needs to be profitable, but profit should not be the main reason for the existence of a business." OK, how out of touch can the Church get? He went on to explain that "Providing fair or just employment and truly fairly serving those who need the products and services of the business is what defines the conduct of business in a Christ-centered world." Well, I don't recall seeing that in any of the McKinsey Key Success Factors: but as quickly as our minds would like to gloss over 'the religious folk and their impracticalities in the face of the real world' I had to recognize that this was right.

The rural center we took on in Zambia—Kavumbu—was intended to be a gratifying and liberating success, both as a site of employment and training for the local people, as well as a platform for community development, healthcare and conservation projects in the area. Also as an exotic vacation destination, it would offer an income source that would allow it to be self-sustaining and allow us to do more. The expected freedom to produce waves of social justice in this part of the world however just never materialized.

Seeking justice in some small patch of the world and being ready to turn around your life to do so isn't by any means a guarantee of success and material abundance; there are some places or projects where we just need to accept this and 'shake off the dust on our sandals' and move on.

It would be nice to conclude with how much more successful and materially blessed we have been since these early beginnings of changing our way of working and living. Well, that's just not what it is about, and that probably isn't what will happen. We're still driving the same old car; and retirement plans are on hold as I feel the need to offer continued real-time support in response to the immediate needs of others (instead of our theoretical future needs). But I dream of God a whole lot more than ever before, trusting that when my cup is trimmed down to size I'll understand that God's generous surplus was always there, and will begin to overflow in service to others as it always should have.

Having a new life-project, I open up to a wholly different spirit (Qi). I develop a craving that seeks with a new heart a visible expression of my determination to turn my life over to love. JustMeQi means: The purpose of my life is to add value to some aspect of every aspect of life.

~ The story of Bill and Katie B

Bill and Katie B were all signed up with Lay Mission Helpers to take their two toddlers on a mission to an as yet undetermined village in Africa. A part of their plan for registering in the program was that they have their house sold so they could be unburdened during their tour of duty. Coincidental to the sale of their house falling out of escrow, Katie became pregnant with their third child.

As a family committed to service, they participated in the *JustFaith²* program at their church to learn of other service options that suited their family life. Via book and video lessons, along with facilitated discussions and community service immersions, Bill and Katie came to a decision: Bill would continue his employment with a charity organization and Katie took the opportunity commit herself more fully to her personal ministry at home as a stay-at-home mother, as well as volunteer at their church school. As a couple, they helped put together a group of parents to spur family activities throughout their community.

I bought lunch today for the lady at the desk in HR while I waited for my new name badge. I don't think anyone has done anything like that for her before. JustMeQi could simply mean I like to pay it forward, like buying coffee for the person in line behind me.

~Denise M

Denise's life plans are being achieved day after day.

She is very proud of her work in nursing, in Red Cross volunteering and as a marathon runner—well, as a half-marathon power-walker.

25 years ago one of her major goals was to have an impact within the community.

Denise: "Our American Red Cross part fills that need. I love nursing and I love the Red Cross. Bringing these two personal passions of mine together is a dream come true. With the help of our excellent PICU staff at the medical center, the future is impacted by the lives we touch today. Plus, the work we do raises awareness for the Red Cross in our community."

Denise: "Every year I am blessed with the opportunity to work on larger format issues, with Red Cross employees and survivors of major disaster events."

JustMeQi means: Never, ever take your voice for granted! Whether it be to tell someone something you need them to know or to voice your opinion. Never say nothing... be heard every day... even if it is only a whisper! This I KNOW!

~Shawn S

In 1996 Shawn S and her friend, AnnaLynda H, decided to get involved in their community by organizing a **Relay For Life** on the campus of the local high School. This is an event originated by the American Cancer Society as a way to involve the local community (schools, churches, businesses and service organizations) in fundraising for research in cancer treatment and care.

Shawn donated the services of her Karaoke company right from the outset. As the principle organizers, Shawn and AnnaLynda contributed "time and talent" more than money or resources. Their creativity and dedication to the cause ended up bringing in uncounted energized and enthused donors, volunteers and participants to what continues to be an annual 24-hour campout and walk to raise money and awareness.

Ultimately Shawn expanded her involvement to multiple sites in the Riverside and San Bernardino, California, areas.

As well, between events, Shawn keeps otherwise busy: She grows her hair long enough to have it trimmed as a donation to the "Locks of Love" program for cancer victims; serves pancake breakfasts to Senior Military Veterans; and brings food and comfort to those in need.

JustMeQi just might mean joining the Peace Corps for a time.

~Bob A & Carol A

After teaching careers that spanned 30 years, Bob and Carol decided to retire to a tour in the Peace Corps. They were in Thailand from January 2006 till April 2008. In Thailand, they worked in a small village near the Cambodian border town of Poipet (across from Aranyaprathet).

Bob & Carol: "We were stationed very close to an area known as the "Killing Fields" as well as the refugee camps set up during the reign of the Khmer Rouge. In 2006, we were the first volunteers to ever work in that area because it had previously been designated as not safe."

Bob: "Carol worked with two high schools teaching English and I worked with two elementary schools (grades 6-8) doing the same. However, our additional projects included teaching the concept of "student-centered activities" to Thai teachers as a way of more actively engaging the students in learning English instead of simply having the students recite in unison."

Additionally, they also conducted student camps where education about HIV and other STD's were emphasized to high school students.

Bob: "We were in Cambodia, from June 2010 to December 2012. Carol was in charge of the training of volunteers and overseeing their projects."

Carol is now Director of Inland Coalition, which is under the umbrella of Reach Out, an NGO that serves the Inland Empire (cities in and around San Bernardino, California) addressing the needs of underrepresented populations.

Carol: "The Inland Coalition's emphasis is providing high school students with an exposure to health careers and creating "pipelines" to help needy students get education for healthcare careers."

Bob: "For now, I stay at home, doing all of the household chores and helping Carol edit her grants and reports and joins her at various volunteer events."

"Good programs are not enough; we don't stop serving until we get our feet under their table."

~Phil H: http://www.ffccsd.org/about-us.aspx

Former mechanical engineer, Phil H first served families in a government run apartment complex. In the beginning, Phil spent his time picking up trash and praying for direction to enable him to furnish more than just the "things" needed by these people.

With associate Tina S, Phil recruited volunteers, and established programs for adult literacy, community sports, after-school homework, and computer mastery as well as an assembly of other programs. Along with a WIC clinic—set-up to provided immunizations for the mothers and children, programs that were started in that community grew to serve countywide and became *Friends and Family Community Connection* (FFCC).

FFCC has a variety of local outreaches from providing dinner for the homeless to collecting and distributing local produce to families in need in the San Diego area.

Sustainability is important to FFCC. Because they understand and don't want to create a dependence on their food or organization, they are working to develop know-how and proficiency in the countries that FFCC serves. Truly, it is a partnership with FFCC. In arrangements with several San Diego based companies, FFCC put together programs that advance the commitment to providing safe water to those in Tanzania and other places in the world who suffer illnesses and sometimes even death due to contaminated water.

FFCC has directed its solar research and design efforts to individual home applications in the form of solar rechargeable lights and solar cell phone chargers. The solar rechargeable LED light provides an equivalent of 300 candle lights and can be used as a wall mount fixture or detached and used as a flashlight. The solar panel is the approximate size of a man's wallet and provides four hours of continuous light. This light will extend a family's day by four hours and provide more time for things like school studies and family interaction."

Fight Against Hunger meals, put together by FFCC volunteers, in point of fact are intended to undo the deleterious effects of starvation in third world countries. One package provides six nutritionally-complete servings to feed starving families around the world as well our own hungry here at home— for pennies a day. Meals are packaged by volunteers at facilities around San Diego County who serve for one hour increments but generate thousands of meals at a time.

Above all, to this day Phil sees to it that FFCC is about building relationships. His programs are just a means to that end.

"May God continue to bless you so that you may continue to bless others."

~Chris and Julianne North: http://buildamiracle.net

Chris and Julianne North met while painting the dormitory of an orphanage and boys home in Tecate, Mexico. At the time, Chris was a graduate of Loyola Marymount University and Julianne was a sophomore there.

Build a Miracle was formed with the idea to gather friends and family and to build one home a year. For their friends, family, neighbors, schoolmates, and fellow parishioners, the excitement about building homes for families living in shacks became contagious.

Since then, they have learned that people are generous; they care and want to help. Given a good program where people truly need help, a program where they can see that they are changing lives, and people will show up where they are needed.

Build a Miracle is a simple program that is changing hundreds of lives on both sides of the border. People in Mexico have a safe and decent place to live. And they have hope. Because people who don't even know them have helped them to have a better life.

How would your life change when you experience the power of giving of yourself to another?

Make your JustMeQi your highest exhilaration.

If excitement is the foremost indicator as to where your Qi will emerge, let joyfulness be your measure. Check out the communities, groups, programs, projects and opportunities that resonate with your Qi. These you'll find will become your priority. You'll relish being full of life. Inspiration will be your stimulation.

If you are taking no more than you are willing to give, you will be at peace. There is the story of children squabbling over the last piece of pie. As the parent is about to cut it in half one child announces that he's taking the bigger piece. "Solomon" then offered to allow one child to do the cutting. Just as the glow hit, he followed with the qualifier that the other child will choose first.

Think of life that way—sometimes you divide the goods, sometimes you choose.

I must realize that mastery is not about perfection. It's about the process—the journey. I am improving when I stay on the path day after day, year after year. Growth comes when I am willing to try, and fail, and try again, for as long as I live.

WHAT'S NEXT?

Where will you go from here for your Just Qi?

Do you long for deeper, more supportive connections with others even though you've spent many years working to better your relationships?

Do you feel pulled to express your gifts and talents in ways that will make a difference, but have no idea how to realize your deeper potentials?

Do you feel called to begin a new project or career that's about service and contribution, but don't know exactly what it might look like?

Are you concerned about the state of our world, yet also feel overwhelmed, confused and powerless to bring about the radical course-correct we all know is needed?

If you answered "Yes" to any of these questions, congratulations! You're probably already living *JustMeQi*.

JustMeQi is the key to making the greatest difference in the world with your gifts, connecting with their inner wisdom, and creating a life of meaning that reflects and expresses who you truly are. You're not alone. When we get involved, we meet others who are conscious, caring and committed to realizing their full potential as well.

Distinct from worldly power, which is the power to create and control things, *JustMeQi* is the power to manifest the very "stuff" that our heart yearns for—familiarity and kinship, communication and meaningfulness, genuine community and the creation of prosperity and success in alignment with our higher values.

In these times, as we grow from survival thinking to mindfulness, part of what we need is to acknowledge is that we can be at home with our true nature of joy and involvement.

My challenge to you is to go to your edge and venture into your *JustMeQi*.

1) Identify your social concerns and objectively evaluate (not emotionally) if they are really real.

    a. What are you concerned about?
    b. Are they local or remote?
    c. Is there danger to fear?

2) What are that most likely consequences of getting involved?
3) Seriously evaluate the impacts of not acting. Are you willing to live with those?
4) Get out of denial about the costs of not deciding to participate in a solution.
5) Is playing it safe effecting your health, or someone else's?

    a. Perhaps the health of a community?
    b. Or the safety of a group?
    c. Or simply a quality of life?

6) Can you expand your capacity to be uncomfortable?

    a. Growth can be terrifying;
    b. Breakthroughs can be messy.

7) Can you strengthen your ability to BE in these uncertain and messy places?
8) Can you build and sustain your sense of self in bigger circumstances?

> a. Will you have the strength, courage and faith that arises from connecting with a new and bigger you?

9) Can you adopt a spirit of adventure and curiosity?
10) Will you throw caution to the wind, and take the JustMeQi leap?

TAKE A STEP

Prime the pump of compassion by taking a leap of faith

Take a step on their behalf.

~Eidelon Cipherest

Set yourself up for *Just* happiness by following a plan that starts from where you are, social-justice-wise, and builds slowly based on how you respond to the growth.

If you're a caring person, but not a regular volunteer, perform good works 2 to 3 times and evaluate the experience. Much like physical training where you would warm up with walking, and then running a bit, at a comfortable speed, try easy service tasks at first. Progress by adding deeper involvement levels or more frequent volunteer intervals.

Check various resources for opportunities: Library bulletin boards, churches, service organizations (Rotary, Kiwanis, Knights of Columbus, etc.), nonprofit groups (American Cancer Society, Autism Society, American Heart Association, etc.), or the internet. Choose an event or activity that you can complete as a one-time involvement (Marathons, fund raisers, festivals or concerts).

Understand this: Life will only give you that which you ask of it. However, don't fail to keep your options open. Always be sensitive to opportunities presented differently than you expected. If your noble intents are legitimate, then the right prospects will become evident in ways that will be meaningful to you, your direct beneficiaries and humanity as a whole.

Expecting your calling to manifest through your church or service organization shouldn't numb you to the knock-upside-the-head from out of the blue. Just when you are relaxing with Facebook or surfing the internet, some posting will whisper your name—don't miss the call. The cookie entrepreneur outside your supermarket may not be calling you to lead a girl-scout troop, but just might be beckoning you to bring a case of cookies to the nearby senior center. The operative word here is "bring." Spend some time with the recipients of your donation.

> *More than a polite "Thank You," gratitude is that deep within you experiencing affection for the focus of your pleasure – it delights like a first kiss or a long embrace.*

Kick start an existence of benevolent order by taking action, step by step, toward an ideal. Small steps at the beginning are less daunting than giant leaps of faith. Cultivate a propensity in a direction and you will be propelled along a focused course. Search out websites related to your ambition. Talk to like-minded people in the area. If possible, visit a locale where a vision similar to yours is being implemented. Join other creators in improving the world. Pray with your heart, your body and your Qi in motion.

How do I add value to the world?

Could it be that you are waiting for someone else to solve the world's problems? Maybe you're praying for government leaders to wave a magic wand and make it all better? Better yet, just maybe it could be that the answer is inside of you, waiting to be recognized or triggered!

JustMeQi will be unlike anything else you have ever considered. It is often discovered as a conversation between the intellect-you, and the spirit-you (*Qi*). As a result, you find yourself as a social entrepreneur and global ally.

In this life, if we were treated according to our *Just* level of merit on any given topic, we would be regarded very different from what would please us. Often we expect treatment based on what we assume someone else received under similar conditions or other subjective circumstance. For many of us, we feel our character is stronger than others. Therefore we judge accordingly.

Social Justice doesn't mean giving-all-to-all without any regard at all. On the other hand, it doesn't mean withholding without regard either. "Will this dollar be used to buy alcohol or food" is a reasonable question—nonetheless, the position of the human before you begs the question as "can I give anyway?"

Take the Time to Get to Know and Love Yourself

If you are pursuing a friendship or relationship, don't you invest time and energy in them? Consider this, have you done so for yourself? In general we fail to really take the time to care for our humanitarian needs. You might be quite fascinated when you begin to delve into your multi-dimensionality.

Here's an idea, try connecting with who you are at your core. Make an effort to understand your personality traits, your basic values, and other aspects—character traits that make you who you are. Cultivating a better relationship with yourself is like getting to know a good friend. Accepting your most valued resource—yourself—will enable you to get in touch with the caring aspect of your being.

Looking at any given, thought-provoking social justice situation, note your feelings in questioning things like: "What is the most giving outcome that I could influence here?"; "How is my own growth challenged by the right response?" Or even "Why should I even care?"

Engage the larger meaning that your response to this testing moment can encompass. Resolve that you will be a prototype of evolution's social potential. Now live from this profounder purpose

Note how your assessment of the situation transforms when you engage it in this manner.

Via *JustMeQi,* deep and powerful personal work is done to advance this attitude and way of being.

If the possibility of practicing *JustMeQi* in your conscious evolution inspires you, then take the journey into an evolutionary relationship with life—people, the planet and, most of all, your spirit. Right now—before reading the next section, take 10 minutes to reflect on the profound significance of your practice of *JustMeQi*. Ask yourself:

- Why do I need to develop myself?
- Why does the world need me to progress? And
- Who are they?

Go deeper than mere intellectual answers, sense for yourself, on all levels, the most genuine answers that come to you.

Once you have it, welcome that resonant inspiration to present itself as you plan your life practice from your heart—from your spiritual you—your very energy being. Contract with yourself from this *Just* intention. Pay attention to the power practice has in living.

When feeling lost, unfulfilled or burned out, don't gaze blankly at the TV or computer screen longing to do something to change things, grab the transition opportunity and actually DO something.

~Eidelon Cipherest

A variation on an often quoted wisdom statement is one that when taken to heart, empowers us all: "Be the wise person who knows what to do next. Be the proficient one knows how to make it happen. Choose to be the virtuous individual who gets it done."

Be mindful of these important life questions: Where am I going? What is my destination? What am I doing to get there?

JustMeQi *means I embrace life's challenges. Just people acknowledge that life is full of good and bad, positive and negative, yet they cultivate a mindset that uses strategies to move the world forward.*

~Eidelon Cipherest

JustMeQi *means Forgiveness is greater than Justice.*

~Eidelon Cipherest

Target collective and individual goals for balancing time and energy to improve activity and stop excuses in their tracks.

Consider trying this line of thinking: "*JustMeQi* means I need to shift my mindset and fully own my responsibilities. If I am going to hit my desired involvement goal, asking for help isn't an option. It's a necessity!"

If you created a "Responsibilities Chart" for detailing chores for a child. Would you expect the child to only follow the letter of the written word? Or would you hope that he/she would learn to "read between the lines" to understand beyond the word—in anticipation?

JustMeQi means I choose to be the kind of person who can get things done. And in getting things done, I love the action, as well as the accomplishment.

Miscellaneous Volunteer ideas:

Volunteer to help bring relief to more seniors who are struggling to meet their basic needs; lead bridge (or any other card games), lead knitting/crocheting/tatting classes, fellowship, group singing or reading.

Employment Retention for corrections re-entry people

Success Projects in the Juvenile and Criminal Justice Systems

Juvenile Justice Behavioral Health Problems, Treatment, and Outcomes in Serious Youthful Offenders—Office of Juvenile Justice and Delinquency Prevention

Second Chance organization to assist newly released prisoners reentering society.

Juvenile Justice Leadership Institute

International Association of Chiefs of Police

Join a group for a special event: Clean the beach, clean a park or a school campus or an underprivileged neighborhood. Volunteer at a fundraiser for a cause you support.

As an outreach to the local community, provide raised garden beds so that the residents can enjoy creative work in herb, ornamental and vegetable gardening.

"Write Letters" as an act of caring for others. Write to seniors, homebound, hospital patients, etc.

If you are good at public speaking, teaching, coordinating volunteers, facilitating meetings, contact various service organizations (i.e. American Cancer Society), various relief programs, hospitals, schools and churches.

Sample list of organizations for ideas that fit your Qi:

Alpha Project, 3737 Fifth Ave, Suite 203, San Diego, CA 92103, (619) 542-1877, info@alphaproject.org: empowers individuals, families, and communities by providing work, recovery and support services to people who are motivated to change their lives and achieve self-sufficiency.

American Cancer Society, 2655 Camino Del Rio N, Suite 100, San Diego, CA 92108

American Cancer Society, Cancer Action Network, 555 11th St, NW, Suite 300, Washington, DC, 20004 1.888.NOW.I.CAN

Bread of Life Rescue Mission, 1919 Apple Street, Suite M, Oceanside, California 92054, 760.722.0800, bolrescue@gmail.com, Serving the Poor and Homeless in North San Diego County

Brother Benno Foundation: 3260 Production Avenue, Oceanside, CA 92058 USA, (760) 439-1244; http://brotherbenno.org

Build a Miracle: http://buildamiracle.net Chris and Julianne North – cjn1@yahoo.com; 619-993-9976; 619-992-0845

Feeding America, Volunteer Programs, volunteersd@feedingamericasd.org, 858.452.3663 x100

Friends & Family Community Connection (FFCC) 12463 Rancho Bernardo Rd PMB #158, SD CA 92128, (858) 204-9643, www.ffccsd.org

Habitat for Humanity, 10222 San Diego Mission Road, San Diego, CA 92108, (619) 283-HOME (4663), www.sdhfh.org

Habitat Restoration Crew, City of San Diego Park and Recreation Department, Meets by the flag poles in front of the Visitor Center. 1 Father Junipero Serra Trail, San Diego, CA 92119

JustFaith Ministries programs help individuals integrate their personal spirituality with social commitment. www.JustFaith.org

Kaiser Permanente Hospice, 10992 San Diego Mission Road, San Diego, CA 92108 Hospice Volunteer; Home Care Volunteer

National City Public Library, 1401 National City Blvd, National City, CA 91950: Volunteer Adult Literacy Tutor

Nile Sisters Development Initiative, 6035 University Ave, Suite 22, San Diego, CA 92115, Refugee Advocate & Case Manager!

Pachamama Alliance, www.pachamama.org, 1009 General Kennedy Avenue | San Francisco, CA 94129, (415)561-4522; a global community that offers people the chance to learn, connect, engage, travel and cherish life for the purpose of creating a sustainable future that works for all.

Rady Children's Hospital, 3020 Children's Way, San Diego, CA 92123

San Diego Organizing Project (SDOP) 4305 University Avenue, Suite 530, San Diego, CA 92105; Phone (619) 285-0797 SDOP.net, a member of PICO organizing, a part of a faith-based movement for justice.

Volunteerism Sources: http://www.volunteermatch.org: Find a Place to Volunteer

ACKNOWLEDGEMENTS

People who contributed stories for JustMeQi

If your body craves attention, you get physically ill. When your Qi needs attention, your body is only one part of you crying out.

In general, we've lost touch with humanity, community and each other. It used to be that communities created a sense of security and belonging for children and adults through common rites and ceremonials. However our detached lifestyles have set individuals—particularly our children—do deal on their own with fears, exasperations and disturbances so they pursue unhealthy and unsafe resources. We all need to know we belong to something bigger than ourselves and that society appreciates the sacredness of life.

Those who serve the tradition of community rituals, as noted in this book, include:

Amy Martinez, Christy Bohan: Individuals donating time to feeding the needy in the community. (Read Amy's story herein)

Bill and Katie Bolstad, (read their story herein)

Bob and Carol Allbaugh, volunteers: (read their story herein)

Bob and Shirley Giese and Phil Harris: Friends and Family Community Connection funding for water purification units to be distributed overseas. (Read Phil's story herein)

Denise Mortati, RN, Loma Linda Medical Center; (read her story herein)

Katie Hodsdon, Sandy Murphy and Marie Revere: Pastoral Care, and a support group for the mentally ill and their families.

Jan Nelte, Pat Caughey and Deacon Joe Santen of Saint James,

Mission Circle: La Colonia de Eden Gardens Youth Camp and Soccer Team and Community Vegetable Garden

Jenny Caughey: CRS Rice Bowls

Joe Gilbreath, **Rise Up Industries.** (Read the RUI story herein)

Maria McEneany and Amanda Maytom; Bi-lateral Safety Corridor Coalition and Project Concern International in San Diego along with several churches, schools and local governments on stemming the flow of human trafficking.

Murray and Amanda Maytom: Global Solidarity. a multi-faceted organization with programs supporting education, Fair Trade, community organizing and social justice. (Read their story herein)

Romela Cummings, RN, homemaker, mother: (read her story herein)

Shawn Salley, volunteer, American Cancer Society: (read her story herein)

Victor Tostado, Manny Aguilar and Amanda Maytom, Community Organizing: working with residential shelters for crime victims, many of whom are teens and domestic workers.

Wayne S. True, M.D., M.P.H., Diplomate American Board of Clinical Lipidology and American Board of Family Medicine, Sharp ReesStealy Medical Group: (read his story herein)

Imagine your name on this list—if not in print, picture it on the list in someone's heart in gratitude for your involvement in making this a better world.

www.ingramcontent.com/pod-product-compliance
Lightning Source LLC
Chambersburg PA
CBHW021124080526
44587CB00010B/629